CountryLiving

Merry & Bright

CountryLiving

Merry  Bright

125 Festive Ideas for Celebrating Christmas

HEARST BOOKS
New York

 # Contents

Foreword

If you're like us, you look forward to the holiday season all year long.

It's such a feast for the senses: the sight of twinkling lights, the

sound of familiar carols, the smell of fresh greens, the taste of warm

gingerbread, the touch of crisp gift wrap and satiny ribbon. Yet for

all the anticipation, it always seems to go by too fast. Surrounded

by a blur of activity, it's easy to lose sight of what matters most—

coming together with family and friends, and being thankful for

what we have. At *Country Living,* we're always on the lookout

for simple, timesaving ways to beautify your home and create

meaningful memories for your family. We are forever inspired by

the homeowners, decorators, artisans, and chefs we feature every

month and, of course, by our own talented staff. *Merry & Bright* is a collection of our favorite ideas for holiday decorating, baking, and crafts. Most require only an hour or an afternoon, so even the busiest among us can incorporate them into our own time-honored traditions. Whether you decide to trim your house from top to bottom or merely to add a new cookie recipe to your repertoire, dozens of festive ideas await you on the pages ahead. From everyone at *Country Living,* we wish you a joyous Christmas!

—The Editors of *Country Living*

Our Gift to You

In the back of this book are eight pages with holiday gift tags. Just cut them out, use a hole punch, and thread onto ribbon.

May your holidays be Merry & Bright!

* ❄ *

Decorating

This is the time of year when the adage "less is more" doesn't necessarily apply, for surely, transforming your home into a magical setting—whether simple or elaborate—is part of what makes the holidays memorable. For many people the holiday season begins with opening boxes of cherished ornaments, glittery tinsel, and festive ribbons and dusting off treasured collections of holiday-themed objects. A beautiful Christmas tree is often the center of attention, but decorating for the holidays also means dressing up tabletops, windowsills, banisters, fireplace mantels, and even the family piano. On the following pages you'll find ideas for creating charming Christmas vignettes and seasonal still lifes, as well as lots of ways to add rustic touches and numerous suggestions for using favorite collections, vintage ornaments, and beloved childhood playthings to great advantage. Whether your take on holiday decorating is traditional or modern, you're sure to find festive inspirations that are perfectly suited to your taste.

Offer a **warm** welcome to holiday guests with any one of these **stylish wreaths.**

· 2

1. Use a wreath to dress up a cupboard door. This lovely, lush wreath is composed of artificial branches that were filled in with real leaves fastened with wire, then adorned with a few personal touches and finished with a satin bow.

2. Christmas in the country lends itself to creative touches of rustic charm. This handmade cedar wreath is decorated with clusters of pepperberry and hydrangea heads, pinecones, pheasant feathers, and a tiny nest of eggs (here filled with robin's egg soaps) and an extravagant organza bow.

3. For an easy mantel embellishment, use a silvery wreath from the craft store and a few diminutive gift boxes.

4. Instead of ornaments, decorate a wreath with apples.

5. Decorate shelves with multiple wreaths and punctuate with jewel-toned ornaments or other trinkets.

· 5

6. Mount a trio of lemon-leaf wreaths around a gilt-framed mirror.

7. To extend the welcome at your front door, lasso a large wreath to a small one with ribbon: Use a slip knot and tie both ends at the top in a big bow.

8. Accent the season with the scent of fresh herbs. This "culinary" wreath is made from bunches of sage, oregano, thyme, and bay leaves.

9. Festoon the front door with a fragrant wreath fashioned from fresh pine, cedar, hydrangea, and green apples.

10. Use roses in your holiday wreath. This tight circle of blossoms is set atop a wreath of moss-covered twigs and rose hips.

Trim the holiday tree with these brilliant ideas ranging from timeless tradition to pure fantasy.

11. Use unexpected colors and patterns to create some Christmas magic. A cocoa-colored pom-pom garland, woven birch-and-rattan spheres, peacock-plumed partridges fashioned from an old patchwork skirt, tartan bows, and flocked-glass balls in warm hues of chocolate and gold offer a pleasing alternative to traditional holiday reds and greens.

12. Use a champagne bucket as a one-of-a-kind tree stand for a small tree. This conifer top (tree tops are often sold by tree farms and vendors) sits in a sterling silver champagne bucket, and is decorated with vivid robin's-egg blue ornaments, small faux birds' nests, and handmade taffeta birds.

13. Inspired by a love of French country antiques, this tree was decorated with silk sunflowers, hydrangeas, peonies, roses, and ribbons.

14. Decorate your tree entirely with handmade ornaments crafted by local artisans. This tree is adorned with cherubs made from beeswax, stars and snowflakes made out of tin, snowflakes and garlands woven with wheat, hand-painted wooden Santas, and translucent hand-blown glass balls.

14

18. For a mix of rustic charm and casual chic, festoon your tree with white feathers, a bird's nest, and mercury glass balls. A snow-topped galvanized bucket holds this spindly tree upright.

19. Use your collections to create one-of-a-kind decorations. Leather-buttoned baby shoes capture the innocence of the season, while three little handmade bears relax near a holiday fir anchored in a Bennington stoneware crock.

20. Celebrate simply. This Douglas fir looks grand adorned exclusively with cut-paper snowflakes. Galvanized geese take on a fanciful air with red ribbon tied around their necks.

21. Vintage letters culled from old signs, printers' type, and alphabet teaching aids festoon this tree. The letters are arranged to spell out holiday words, such as "ho ho ho" and "holly." The red-and-green color scheme emphatically says "Christmas."

22. Everyone has his own preference for a fresh tree: For hanging ornaments, the sturdiest branches belong to the blue spruce. Firs are the most fragrant and long lasting. Scotch pines hold their needles even when dry.

Decorate every corner of the house with all that delights you.

·23

23. Use pastry tins as candleholders for glitter-dusted votives.

24. Use a white palette for a sense of serenity. Pillar candles, a garland of pearl buttons, and a wrought-iron mirror lend a romantic feel to this mantel.

25. A banister offers ample opportunity for imaginative holiday adornment. Use satin ribbons, strings of beads, and garlands of greenery.

26. For a finishing touch to your banister decorations, prop a teddy bear with a sleigh bell on the newel post.

27. Wind a garland up a banister. Wire together real fruit, such as limes, small apples, pears, and lemons (they'll last for about two weeks), secure them at intervals to the newel post, and finish with lustrous satin ribbon.

28. Use children's toys to create an enchanting holiday display. Here, a Victorian child's wooden wagon holds a handcrafted teddy bear and reproductions of a folk art china doll and dollhouse.

29. Create a nostalgic farm vignette around the base of a small tree. Here, two charming scenes surround this tabletop tree, one on the table and one on the floor.

30. Stage a sweet holiday farm scene on the mantel or atop a cupboard with a herd of antique German sheep and a lighted cabin.

31. Look around your home for unusual display pieces. This pair of ironstone gravy boats makes perfect planters, especially when brightened by a silver platter base.

32. In lieu of a wreath, hang a basket filled with greenery and a charming Santa figure on the door.

33. Place vases and urns filled with greenery throughout the house. This iron urn holds juniper, cedar, and balsam branches.

34. A mixture of indoor and outdoor items makes for a refreshingly unconventional mantel arrangement.

35. The beauty of pinecones makes them an ideal decoration during the holidays. Here, a garland made out of pinecones frames a fireplace, and pinecones in urns grace the mantel.

36. Looking to add some dazzle to your home this holiday season? Gold, in all its luster, offers a brilliant alternative to traditional garnet and green. The wreath and garland around this fireplace are festooned with gold ornaments and dappled with gold paint, while old-fashioned white feather trees decorated with gold ornaments brighten the hearth.

37. For an elegantly rustic look, trim the mantel with a simple garland of evergreen and berries and a row of stockings made with vintage fabrics.

38. Some pieces of furniture are ideal for decorating. A piano stands in for a mantel as the perfect place to hang stockings and top with a collection of birdhouses and greenery.

39. Tuck a pair of wee animals—stuffed teddy bears, small dogs, or a sheep or two—into a stocking and hang from a doorknob, mantel, or other prominent spot.

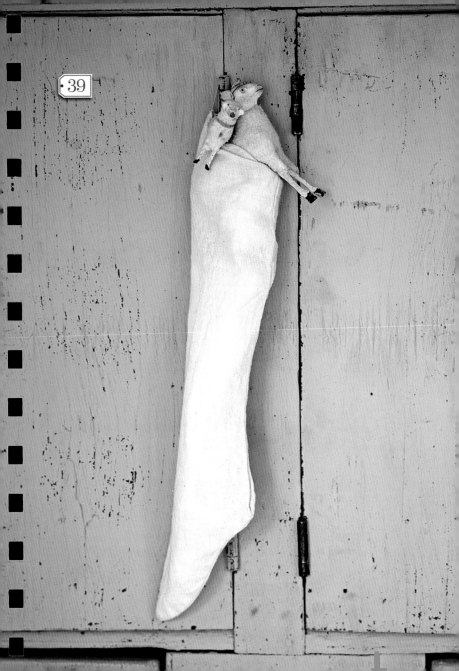

40. Use a coffee cup to serve up a seasonal display.

41. Prop vintage postcards in antique florists' frogs.

42. Decorate a doorknob with a papier-mâché cone filled with silk flowers.

43. Make little touches as much a part of the holidays as elaborate ones. Charm guests in the powder room with a tarnished compote brimming with pearly baubles—a subtle bow to the season.

44. Transform a bowl of pretty pears perched on a bed of boxwood into a lovely centerpiece by tying velvet bows onto their stems.

45. Make fragrance a part of your holiday décor. This small tree made of boxwood sprigs stuck in damp florist's foam is decorated with orange-clove pomanders and a garland of dried rose hips.

46

46. Arrange bunches of fresh herbs, lavender, dried orange slices, and soft clumps of moss on a serving platter to fill your home with the aroma of a holiday potpourri.

·47

47. Create a holiday display inside a small cabinet by replacing everyday items with angel figurines and apples.

48. Transform the mantel into a festive stage by pairing vintage ornaments with a collection of antique bottles. Green and gold French and German hand-painted ornaments (including some in a rare teardrop shape) resemble jeweled stoppers perched atop early twentieth-century glass bottles.

·48

Add holiday **sparkle** to any room with these **ornament ideas.**

·49

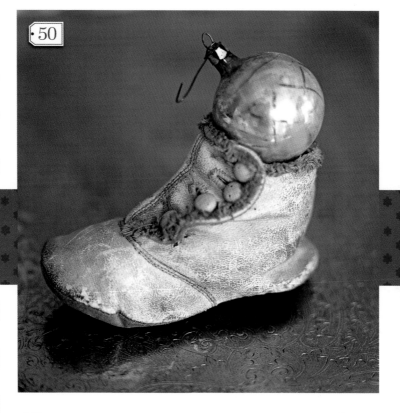

49. Even childhood playthings can be incorporated into your holiday décor. In an antique English transferware compote, a lovingly worn teddy bear embraces a vintage ornament, exuding the sweetness of the season.

50. Create a delicate still life by pairing an heirloom ornament with a baby shoe, evoking a wistful nostalgia for times gone by.

51. To show off a collection of vintage glass balls or other special ornaments, place them in paper candy and cupcake cups and display on a favorite plate.

52. Age ornaments by exposing them to the elements. These ornaments achieved their pearly patina after sitting in a garden for six months where they served as miniature gazing globes. The unpolished champagne bucket boasts a mottled tarnish that perfectly complements the cool luster of the ornaments.

·52

54

53. Whether crimson, scarlet, or burgundy, red captures the eye. In a white hallway, a wire urn filled with shiny red ornaments becomes an instant focal point.

54. Make your collections come alive by displaying them in unexpected ways. A collection of colored-glass balls in canning jars can be placed anywhere a touch of color is needed.

55. For a charming centerpiece or tabletop decoration, cluster a group of diminutive animal figurines on a white plate or serving platter. Place an ornament in the center.

56. Use children's toys to decorate a windowsill, the fireplace mantel, under the tree, or anywhere that could use a spot of holiday cheer. An antique fire engine, a teddy bear, or beloved doll can add a touch of nostalgia to any nook or cranny.

57. No room left on the mantel? You can always find another spot to display your holiday collections. Here, a contingent of Santas made of all manner of materials convenes on a kitchen table, where some are supported by picnic hampers covered in scarlet tartan. Above them hangs a wreath, to which a quirky selection of found objects was glued.

58. Group holiday ornaments and other treasures in your prettiest bowls and pots. Here, in a sturdy English ironstone bowl, simple silver and gold balls are clustered in a nest of yard-sale tinsel.

59. For a display that sparkles, fill a milk-glass compote with a collection of vintage glass ornaments.

60. Use ribbon to hang a collection of ornaments in a window. Here, we've chosen sky blue organza.

Entertaining & Tabletop Decorating

One of the greatest joys of the holidays is spending time with family and friends. Sitting around a fireplace, hosting parties, or gathering around the table to savor a special meal, share stories, and revel in the welcoming atmosphere is what the season is all about. Whether you're offering a light afternoon buffet or a six-course extravaganza, set a festive scene: Grace the table with your most luxurious linens and put out lots of glowing candles. Create an enchanting centerpiece and accessorize each place setting with a seasonal name card and napkin rings. An artful arrangement of mix-and-match tableware reflects a casual chic, while using heirloom china and crystal sets a rich, elegant tone. Cherished collections can be used as centerpieces, either on their own or adorned with ribbons and other embellishments. And why not bring the outdoors in by using greenery as part of a centerpiece or to embellish place cards? After all, this is the time of year to gather 'round to eat, drink, and be merry!

Treasures **old** and **new** share the tabletop spotlight.

· 61

62

61. White on white can be magical. Here, three white pedestal stands are stacked one atop the other and crowned with a charming white snow figure.

62. Gather a collection of dazzling baubles in a serving platter to create a sparkling stage for a tabletop tree. Here, a small statue of Our Lady of Grace presides over a collection of silver, gold, and blue ornaments in a vintage platter set atop a silver tray.

63. For a dessert buffet, vary the heights of serving pieces with pedestal cake stands, either alone or stacked to create tiers.

64. The busy holiday season gives us countless reasons to gather together with family and friends. Invite guests to stop by your home after a school concert, ice skating, or Christmas dinner for a sweet finale of desserts and refreshments.

70. Gather an assortment of Victorian Christmas lights in a compote or on a cake stand for a festive holiday centerpiece.

71. Use a pair of berry-studded topiaries in antique urns as centerpieces on a buffet table.

72. Fill a row of glass vases with red roses for centerpieces. Shimmering glass dominates this simple but elegantly dressed table.

·68

67. Pair fresh-cut flowers in a single, unexpected color—pink, for example—with antique silver and mercury glass for an elegant presentation.

68. Infuse your holiday gathering with nostalgia by displaying vintage ornaments and figurines. Chenille tabletop trees and a candy-coated color scheme bring this dining room to life.

69. You can always depend on candles to create captivating and inexpensive focal points on your holiday table.

·67

65. A graceful footed candy dish or compote made from pewter or blown glass is the ideal presentation for old-fashioned ribbon candy. Embellish the arrangement with sprigs of evergreen and place in an easy-to-reach spot.

66. Create a tasty centerpiece for your dining table or buffet: Stack a graduated trio of footed glass compotes. Secure each pedestal to the next larger one with florist's putty, and fill the bowls with festive candies.

Make **merry** with family and friends around a beautiful
holiday table.

·73·

Enchant with festively wrapped party favors.

·82

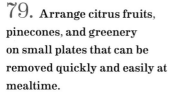

79. Arrange citrus fruits, pinecones, and greenery on small plates that can be removed quickly and easily at mealtime.

80. Pewter chargers (these are Early American reproductions) add an old-fashioned feel to the holiday table. The dinner napkin is simply tied with a red ribbon and a sprig of greenery.

81. Add a golden touch to your place settings. White china rimmed with gold stands out against gold chargers while jingle bells add a festive note to each guest's plate. Tiny pinecones accented with gold serve as place-card holders.

77. Tagged with guests' names and placed in ironstone butter pats, small ornaments can serve as place cards on the holiday table (and afterwards, can go home with the guests as party favors).

78. Attach a name tag to a Victorian Christmas light for a personalized place card at your holiday dinner.

75. There are myriad ways to infuse your holiday place settings with accents from the outdoors. A crimson Lady apple (from the grocery store) gains luster when given a dusting of glitter and creatively embellished with a small red bird.

76. Personalize a place setting by using a gold glitter pen to monogram an ornament, napkin, or place card.

73. Bring the frosty elegance of the winter world indoors with your table settings. Here, evoking the bright seasonal landscape, snowy whites and earthy browns team up with sky blues and winterberry reds. The white cotton cloth creates a pristine base for bottle-brush trees, pinecone place-card holders, and tableware with naturalistic motifs. Bell jars borrowed from the garden sparkle.

74. Place-card holders good enough to eat may not last the meal. Here, snowflake-shaped cookies with dainty touches of icing suggest the delicious fare ahead. Large cookies (from a bakery or your favorite recipe) are less likely to break—or disappear— before dessert.

Colorful papers, rainbow ribbons, and other whimsical touches turn presents into presentations.

·85

Crafts

Homemade trimmings are cherished for the dear memories they hold, and there is nothing like a handmade decoration to show friends and loved ones how much you care. You needn't be an expert crafter to make a special holiday decoration for your home or to give to a loved one. To craft a card, stocking, or wreath, or to add a touch of whimsy—or elegance—to a wrapped package, all that's required is a little time and imagination. Simple green wreaths can be transformed into one-of-a-kind pieces by attaching ribbons, flowers, birds' nests, or childhood keepsakes. Colorful ribbons, old buttons, or materials from the outdoors, such as a wisp of greenery or a cluster of small pinecones, can be fashioned into ornaments or added to wrapped presents. On the pages that follow, you will find fabulous ideas for gift wrapping, wreath-making, and ornament crafting that range from rustic to simple to sophisticated and that reflect the magic of this joyful season.

82. Tuck party favors or small gifts inside paper cones, each with its own handcrafted gift tag attached, and present them gathered together in a large white basket.

83. Dish out diminutive party favors from an elegant serving vessel, such as this compote of textured milk glass. Tiny scalloped name tags hang on silver elastic strings.

84. Fill take-out containers with nests of tissue paper or raffia and tuck treats—chocolates, an ornament, or a little toy—inside. Secure each box with a colorful ribbon tied in a bow and stack on a cake stand until guests depart.

85. Embellish your gifts with a seashell instead of a traditional bow.

86. For a bit of Old World charm, wrap presents in sheet music or photocopied pages from vintage books. Used-book stores often carry inexpensive music and volumes that are damaged but retain usable individual sheets. Choosing favorite composers or authors will personalize the gifts.

87. When packing presents to mail or to carry, bows can get crushed. Instead of using a bow, affix a beautiful card to the wrapping paper.

88. PAPER GIFT CYLINDERS

**A handmade box is as much a present as what's inside.
To craft these gift boxes you'll need:**

Fabric or wallpaper to photocopy
Card stock
Glue stick
Lightweight cardboard
Ribbon for hanging loop
Ruler and pencil
Small round object to trace
Straight and scallop-edged scissors

To make: Photocopy a piece of fabric or wallpaper onto card stock.
Measure and cut lengthwise a strip the desired height of the box,
then glue the ends together to form a cylindrical body. Trace a round
object slightly larger than the opening of the body to make the top
and bottom, and cut each piece with scallop-edged scissors. From the
cardboard, cut 4 strips, each about 2 inches long by ½ inch wide, and
fold each in half. Positioning them at equal intervals, glue one half of
each strip to the inside bottom of the box and the other half against
the inside of the body—thus adhering the bottom to the body. Cut a
small hole in the top of the box; for a handle, fold a piece of ribbon in
half, pass the fold up through the hole and knot the ends under the
box top. Fill the box with lightweight treats.

89. Use brown paper and red string, tied in a variety of ways, plus an exquisite ornament to create a memorable presentation.

90. Personalize gift tags with rubber stamps, holiday stickers, and other items available in stationery and craft stores. Secure each to a box using a length of vintage ribbon, bakery string, or jewel-toned embroidery thread.

91. Make a felt gift bag. Cut two rectangles of felt (use two different colors); stitch the rectangles together on three sides, leaving one side open. Tuck a present into the bag and tie it shut with ribbon. Or make an envelope by cutting one rectangle several inches longer than the other rectangle to create a flap that can be folded over. Scallop the top edge of the flap and secure with a button or ribbon. Decorate with felt cutouts.

Deck the halls with **handmade** holiday **decorations**.

·92

92. Transform worn cashmere sweaters into the prettiest stockings ever. Start with a purchased pattern or draw your own.

93. Use your fabric scraps to create one-of-a-kind stockings. Jester-style cuffs add to the fun.

94. If your collection of ornaments has grown beyond what your Christmas tree can accommodate, create a wreath: Use a hot glue gun to secure ornaments of all sizes and colors to a polystyrene wreath form (available at craft stores), then hang with a ribbon.

· 95

95. Create a dazzling centerpiece by gluing colorful beads to a plain pillar candle, then surround it with glittered ornaments affixed with glue to a cardboard wreath form.

96

96. Make a pinwheel wreath out of the funny papers. To make a pinwheel, take a newspaper square and, beginning at each corner, make a cut toward (but not all the way through) the center, forming four triangles. Bring one corner of each triangle to the center of the square and secure with glue. Adhere the finished pinwheels to a round Styrofoam wreath base.

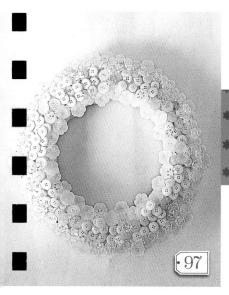

·97

·98

97. Dip into your button collection and make an all-white button wreath. All you need is a wreath form, buttons, and a hot glue gun.

98. Instead of a traditional holiday wreath on the front door, try a silvery cone of metal bells embellished with a beautifully tied bow. Working from the bottom up, use florists' pins to fasten small bells to an inverted triangle of Styrofoam. Top with a bow fashioned from extra-wide ribbon.

99. Fashion a rustic star ornament. With a craft knife, cut a star from a birch bark sheet. Glue twigs painted gold to the bark; wind 20-gauge gold wire around one point, then twist to secure it on the branch.

100. Create a pinecone tree. Anchor a cone-shaped foam base in a container. Wire the cones onto 2-inch wooden floral picks. Insert picks downward into the foam, starting at the bottom with the largest cones. Conceal the foam by tucking sheet moss among the pinecones.

101. To make a peanut ring for your wild bird neighbors, thread unshelled peanuts at their narrowest point onto a length of thin galvanized wire (for a large ring, you'll need about 15 inches of wire). Bend the wire to form a circle, then twist the ends together tightly to secure them. Hang the ring with household twine.

102. BERIBBONED TREES

Create a tabletop "forest" of these fanciful conical ribbon-wrapped "trees." You'll need:

Straight pins with decorative heads, especially 2-inch corsage pins

Ribbons in assorted widths, several yards per cone

Styrofoam cones, assorted sizes up to 24 inches tall

Braid and trim

Beads and other faux jewels

To make: With a straight pin, secure one end of a ribbon to the top of a cone. Overlapping the edges, wrap the ribbon diagonally around the cone, fastening with pins every 4 inches or as needed to keep smooth. If you need to add another length of ribbon, fold under its starting end. When the cone is covered, secure the end of the ribbon with a pin under the base.

To embellish the cones, skewer beads with corsage pins and use to affix festive trims (like these snowflakes or braids), or decorate randomly. For the best results, insert pins into the cone at a slightly downward angle. Add pearls, beads, baubles, and other sparkling embellishments as lavishly as desired. For a touch of chic, decorate the top—a fancy hatpin makes a stellar topper! To finish, pin a border of fringe, braid, or trim along the base. Stand the tree on its base, or place it on a pedestal for extra height.

104. Give the gift of scent. Make a paper cone from construction paper that you first decorate with stickers or rubber stamps; secure the shape with tape or glue. Cut a piece of tulle to fit inside, and fill with lavender. Punch two holes at the top and string a ribbon through them for hanging.

103. Fabric-Wrapped Balls

Use your collection of fabric scraps to craft rag ball ornaments.
You will need:

Straight pins
Fabric strips of any kind
Styrofoam balls (all one size or in a variety of sizes)
Felt shapes (cut them yourself or purchase them at a fabric shop)
Small beads
Ribbon or trim for hanging loops

To make: Insert a pin through a strip of fabric at a starting point on a ball. Wrap the strip around the ball, using pins at intervals to hold it in place. Add more strips as needed, until the ball is completely covered. You can wrap the fabric in a random pattern or arrange it in a more orderly design. To embellish the balls with felt shapes, first thread a bead onto a pin; then push the pin through the felt shape into the ball. Attach a loop of ribbon or trim to the top of the ball with a pin.

105. Make a star garland. Cut one star for a template, then cut out as many more as desired from card stock. Punch a small hole in the center of each star and string with thin twine. Drape around a tree, across a window, or along a banister.

·105

106. Embellish plain pillar candles. Using a hot glue gun or tiny pushpins, decorate with berries, holly leaves, glitter, confetti, cinnamon sticks, or pine needles.

·107

107. To make simple Christmas "crackers," gather cardboard paper rolls, fill with trinkets, wrap in newsprint, and tie the ends with ribbon. They may not pop when opened, but they will spill with goodies.

108. Bring a sense of the past to your home by handcrafting folk-art decorations. To make these votives, tape a small paper tree to the glass, spray the entire glass with glue, and roll it in artificial snow or glitter so that it looks frosted. When the paper is removed, the tree will be transparent, allowing a colored candle within to glimmer through. After the holidays, the Christmas motif can be washed off with hot, soapy water.

·108

109. Let it snow! Assure yourself a flurry of snowflakes by getting a little crafty with tissue paper and scissors. No time to snip? Ask an artistic friend to help, or use store-bought paper snowflakes. To display them in the window, spritz the panes (inside the house) with water using a plant mister or a recycled spray bottle filled with plain water. Place the cutouts on the misted window and voilà! The faux flakes look festive from inside or out and will stay in place for weeks.

110. APPLE KISSING BALL

Steal a smooch! Composed of Lady apples and fresh cranberries mounted on a sphere of Styrofoam and dusted with sparkling sugar, this easy-to-make arrangement will delight for weeks. You will need:

Ribbon, about 1 yard
Styrofoam ball, 8 or 10 inches in diameter
Floral picks (with wire removed) and toothpicks
40 Lady apples (approximately)
60 fresh cranberries (approximately)
2 egg whites, lightly beaten
1 cup sugar

To make: Tie the ribbon into a bow at one end. Use a letter opener or chopstick to feed the other end of the ribbon through the center of the ball. Secure the ribbon by inserting a floral pick at the bow knot.

Push the blunt end of a floral pick a quarter of the way into the bottom of a Lady apple, then push the pointed end all the way into the ball. Cover the entire ball with apples, then spear cranberries onto toothpicks and fill in the spaces. Use a pastry brush to paint the apples and cranberries with the egg whites. Place on a baking rack for about 15 minutes, or until the egg white is nearly dry but still tacky. Sprinkle sugar over the entire surface of the ball, turning as necessary; leave on the rack until dry. Shake off the excess sugar, hang the ball over a doorway, and enjoy!

Baking

Cookie-baking is a cherished holiday tradition, and come December, visions of fanciful cookies become a reality. For many of us, it simply wouldn't be Christmas without them, as they're often the high point at holiday gatherings and make tempting presents for favorite teachers and neighbors alike. You can make a gift of cookies even more memorable by packing them in distinctive containers. Arrange them in a vintage lunchbox, tuck them into a colorfully decorated cigar box or old candy tin, or slip them into individual bags festively tied with ribbon. Elegantly wrapped cookies also make sweet party favors, allowing guests to prolong their enjoyment of a holiday gathering. In this chapter we offer recipes and wrapping ideas for an enticing selection of the season's best-loved cookies. Enjoy their tempting aroma and buttery flavor, but be sure to leave some for Santa on Christmas Eve. After all, cookies are what sweet memories are all about.

Tuck homemade treats in pretty packaging.

·111

STARS
2 CUPS UNS~
1¼ CUPS S~
2 TBLP VAN~
¾ TSP ~
CREAM
SUGAR, ~
YOLKS, ~ ~ FL~
TO LOW, ADD FL~ IN HALF
DIVIDE DOUGH, WRAP, AT 3X
INTO A RECTANGLE. BAKE AT 3X
CUT OUT STARS. * BAKE A
~24HR
TE.

·112

111. Create a personalized gift bag. Stack cutout cookies in a baking cup encircled with a matching ribbon. Place the filled cup into a "cello" bag and, using pinking shears, make a zigzag cut across the top of the bag. String a copy of the recipe and a glittery initial of the recipient on a ribbon and secure to the bag with a bow.

112. Nestle a gift of homemade cookies and cookie cutters in a tea towel inside a pretty tin—this green-and-white, picnic-plaid example suits the festive season.

113. Make your baked gift extra special by including a handmade or computer-designed recipe card.

114. Use a vintage lunchbox tied with a pretty bow and greenery to "wrap" a gift of cookies.

115. As an alternative to traditional paper cards, present friends and loved ones with edible decorated Christmas-tree "cards." Package them in clear cellophane envelopes fastened with festive ribbon bows.

116. To keep baked goods fresh when shipping, wrap in foil or plastic wrap; be sure to label before packing. Cookies or bars should be individually wrapped or packed in layers with waxed paper or tissue in between.

'Tis the season for
baking holiday cookies.

·117

117. Coconut-Cookie Favors

Send guests home with delectables set in silver paper cups, individually wrapped in cellophane, and tied up with satin ribbons. *Makes 2 dozen cookies*

2 cups sweetened flaked coconut
$\frac{1}{4}$ cup sugar
$1\frac{1}{2}$ tablespoons all-purpose flour
4 tablespoons butter ($\frac{1}{2}$ stick), melted
2 large egg yolks
1 large egg

To make: Preheat the oven to 350°F. Line a baking sheet with parchment paper. Set aside. Toss the coconut, sugar, flour, butter, egg yolks, and egg together in a large bowl. Mix well. With wet hands, form the mixture into walnut-size balls, and place on the prepared baking sheet. Bake until lightly golden—about 12 to 15 minutes. Transfer the cookies to wire racks to cool completely.

118. Lemon Meringue Cookies

For formal parties, use an antique compote or crystal punch bowl to display your most special sweets to spectacular effect. Our meringue cookies, tinted with edible sparkling dust, emulate the shape and glow of vintage ornaments. *Makes about 3 dozen cookies*

6 large egg whites, at room temperature
2 teaspoons fresh lemon juice
$\frac{1}{8}$ teaspoon salt
1 teaspoon lemon extract
1 teaspoon vanilla extract
$1\frac{1}{4}$ cups sugar

1. Make the meringues: Preheat the oven to 200°F. Line 2 baking sheets with parchment paper. Combine the egg whites, lemon juice, and salt in a large bowl, and beat using a mixer set on low speed until foamy. Add the extracts, increase the mixer speed to medium, and add the sugar in a slow, continuous stream. Increase speed to medium-high and continue to beat until stiff peaks form.

2. Bake the cookies: Transfer the meringue to a large pastry bag fitted with a large star tip. Pipe 3-inch-long "S" shapes on the prepared baking sheets. Bake, without opening the oven, for 1 hour. Reduce the temperature to 175°F and continue to bake for 2 more hours or until the cookies are completely dry. Transfer the cookies, on the parchment paper, to wire racks to cool completely. Store in an airtight container for up to 1 week.

119. Holiday Cookie Cards

This holiday season, send cookie greeting cards packed in decorative, durable boxes that can remain a keepsake long after the cookies have been savored. *Makes 8 cookies*

4 large egg whites
1 cup sugar
1 cup all-purpose flour
$\frac{1}{2}$ cup unsalted butter (1 stick), melted and cooled
$1\frac{1}{2}$ teaspoons ground aniseed
$\frac{1}{2}$ teaspoon vanilla extract

1. Make the batter: Whisk the egg whites and sugar together in a medium bowl until combined. Add the flour, butter, aniseed, and vanilla, and whisk until smooth. Cover with plastic wrap and refrigerate for 1 to 24 hours.

2. Bake the cookies: Preheat the oven to 350° F. Cut out 8 strips of paper, each 10 inches long by $\frac{1}{2}$ inch wide; write your desired holiday messages on them, and set aside. On a nonstick baking sheet or baking sheet lined with a nonstick silicone mat, spread 3 tablespoons batter into an 8-inch round. Bake until lightly browned—about 7 minutes. Cool slightly, but make sure the cookie remains warm and pliable. Use a spatula to lift the cookie from the pan and turn it over. Place one of the prepared message strips in the center of the cookie and gently fold the cookie in half to form a semicircle; do not flatten or crease the fold. Bend the 2 ends of the straight edge of the cookie in towards each other. Hold the cookie in this position until set; then transfer to a wire rack to cool completely. Repeat this process 7 times with the remaining batter. Store in an airtight container for up to 3 days.

120. Coffee-Cream Sandwiches

Sweet to eat, and if imaginatively presented, just as sweet to remember. *Makes about 4 dozen cookies*

1 large egg

$\frac{2}{3}$ cup all-purpose flour

$\frac{1}{3}$ cup granulated sugar

$2\frac{1}{2}$ tablespoons unsalted butter, melted and cooled

$\frac{3}{4}$ teaspoon baking powder

$\frac{1}{2}$ teaspoon vanilla extract

2 tablespoons instant espresso powder

2 teaspoons boiling water

$\frac{1}{2}$ cup unsalted butter (1 stick), softened

2 cups confectioners' sugar, sifted

$\frac{1}{2}$ cup plus 2 tablespoons mascarpone

1. Make the cookies: Combine the egg, flour, granulated sugar, butter, baking powder, and vanilla in a medium bowl. Beat using a mixer set on low speed until smooth—about 1 minute. Following the manufacturer's instructions, make the cookies in a preheated pizzelle iron: Use a generous $\frac{1}{4}$ teaspoonful of batter per cookie and cook for 45 seconds to 1 minute. (Be careful: Unwatched batter will burn quickly.) Lift the cookie from the iron and transfer to a wire rack to cool completely. Repeat with the remaining batter.

2. Make the filling: Dissolve the espresso powder in the water and let cool. Using a mixer set on medium speed, cream the softened butter in a medium bowl until smooth. Add the confectioners' sugar and continue to beat until fluffy. Add the espresso mixture and beat to incorporate. Stir in the mascarpone.

3. Assemble the cookies: Place 2 teaspoonfuls filling between 2 cookies. Repeat with the remaining filling and cookies. Store in an airtight container for up to 3 days.

121. CHECKERBOARD COOKIES

Checkerboard cookies look difficult to make, but they really aren't. It is simply a matter of slicing and stacking the layers of chocolate and vanilla dough. Once you try making them, you are sure to get hooked! *Makes 6 dozen cookies*

5 cups all-purpose flour, sifted
¼ teaspoon salt
2 cups unsalted butter (4 sticks), softened
1 cup sugar
2 large eggs
2 teaspoons vanilla extract
3 tablespoons Dutch-processed unsweetened cocoa
1 large egg white

·121

1. Make the dough: Combine the flour and salt in a medium bowl. Set aside. Beat the butter in a large bowl using a mixer set on medium-high speed until light and creamy. Gradually add the sugar and continue to beat until light and fluffy. Add the eggs one at a time, beating well after each addition. Add the vanilla. Reduce the mixer speed to low and beat in the flour mixture until a dough forms. Remove half the dough and set aside. Mix the cocoa into the remaining dough until fully incorporated. Pat the vanilla and the chocolate dough each into an 11- by 9-inch rectangle. Wrap each in plastic wrap and refrigerate until firm.

2. Make the checkerboards: Brush the vanilla dough with egg white and place the chocolate dough on top. Press gently and cut in half lengthwise. Brush one half with egg white and stack the remaining half on top, making certain the vanilla and chocolate doughs alternate. Cut the resulting stack in half lengthwise. Set one half aside. Slice the other one into thirds lengthwise and turn the middle section upside down. Lightly brush the adjacent sides with egg white and gently press together to form a checkerboard-patterned log. Repeat with the set-aside dough stack. Wrap each log in plastic wrap and refrigerate until firm.

3. Bake the cookies: Preheat the oven to 350° F. Line 2 baking sheets with parchment paper. Slice 1 checkerboard log crosswise into ¼-inch-thick cookies. Place 1 inch apart on the prepared baking sheets and bake, rotating the sheets halfway through, until firm—12 to 15 minutes. Transfer the cookies to wire racks to cool completely. Store in an airtight container for up to 1 week.

122. Holiday Blondies

Simple ingredients ensure that these cookies are engagingly festive: a topping of puffed cereal sweetened with caramel turns this everyday blondie into a memorable treat. *Makes 16 squares*

1 cup all-purpose flour

$\frac{1}{2}$ teaspoon baking powder

$\frac{1}{2}$ teaspoon salt

1 cup firmly packed light brown sugar

6 tablespoons unsalted butter ($\frac{3}{4}$ stick), melted and cooled slightly

1 large egg

2 large egg yolks

2 teaspoons vanilla extract

6 tablespoons chocolate-hazelnut spread, such as Nutella

$3\frac{1}{2}$ cups Kix brand cereal

1 cup granulated sugar

$\frac{1}{4}$ cup water

$\frac{1}{4}$ teaspoon fresh lemon juice

·122

1. Make the cookie crust:
Preheat the oven to 350°F. Line the bottom of a 10-inch-square pan with parchment paper. Set aside. Sift the flour, baking powder, and salt together into a medium bowl. Set aside. Whisk the brown sugar, butter, egg, egg yolks, and vanilla together in a medium bowl. Add the sugar mixture to the flour mixture and mix until well combined. Spread the dough in the bottom of the prepared pan. Bake until the edges are lightly browned—about 13 minutes. Cool in the pan on a wire rack for 15 minutes. Invert onto the wire rack, lift off the pan, and cool completely.

2. Assemble the cookies: Dollop the chocolate-hazelnut spread over the crust and smooth with a spatula; cut into 16 squares. Place the cereal in a large bowl. Set aside. Fill a large bowl with ice water. Set aside. Combine the granulated sugar, water, and lemon juice in a heavy small saucepan, and cook over high heat until the mixture turns a light caramel color—about 10 minutes. Dip the bottom of the pan into the ice water to stop the cooking, then pour 6 to 8 tablespoons of the caramel onto the cereal. Toss until well coated, adding more caramel if necessary. Working quickly, form the cereal into small clusters and place on the cookie squares. Drizzle with the remaining caramel and let cool completely. Store, in a single layer, in an airtight container for up to 5 days.

123. Spritz Cookies

Buttery spritz cookies are a holiday classic. Half the fun when making them is choosing which cookie template to press the cookies through. *Makes about 6 dozen cookies*

2 cups all-purpose flour
¼ teaspoon baking powder
¼ teaspoon salt
1 cup unsalted butter (2 sticks), softened
½ cup sugar
2 large egg yolks
2 teaspoons vanilla extract
2 teaspoons grated lemon zest

1. Make the dough: Sift the flour, baking powder, and salt together into a medium bowl. Set aside. Beat the butter in a large bowl with a mixer set on medium speed until creamy. Add the sugar in a slow stream and continue beating until incorporated. Add the egg yolks, vanilla, and lemon zest and beat thoroughly. Reduce the mixer speed to medium-low and add the flour mixture, beating until a smooth and pliable dough forms. Wrap the dough in plastic wrap and refrigerate for 30 minutes.

2. Bake the cookies: Preheat the oven to 350°F. Following manufacturer's instructions, fill a cookie press with some of the dough and fit the press with a decorative template. Press the cookies, 1 inch apart, onto an ungreased baking sheet. Bake until the edges are browned—10 to 12 minutes. Transfer the cookies to wire racks to cool completely. Repeat with the remaining dough to make more cookies. Store in an airtight container for up to 1 week.

124. Sugar-Cookie Stars

Dangle these sugar-cookie stars from miniature trees and invite visitors to help themselves. *Makes about 6 dozen cookies*

5 cups all-purpose flour

2 teaspoons ground nutmeg

$\frac{1}{2}$ teaspoon salt

2 cups unsalted butter (4 sticks), softened

1$\frac{1}{4}$ cups sugar

2 large eggs

3 large egg yolks

2 teaspoons vanilla extract

2 tablespoons grated orange zest

1 tablespoon heavy cream

·124

1. Make the dough: Sift the flour, nutmeg, and salt together into a medium bowl. Set aside. Beat the butter in a large bowl using a mixer set on medium speed until creamy. Add the sugar in a steady stream and continue to beat until incorporated. Add the eggs, 2 of the egg yolks, the vanilla, and orange zest, and beat thoroughly. Reduce the mixer speed to medium-low, add the flour mixture, and beat until combined. Divide the dough in half, shape each piece into a 6-by 4-inch rectangle, and wrap in plastic wrap. Refrigerate for 4 to 24 hours.

2. Cut out the cookies: Preheat the oven to 350°F. Line 2 baking sheets with parchment paper. Set aside. On a lightly floured surface, roll out the dough to $\frac{1}{8}$-inch thickness. Using cookie cutters of your choice, cut out shapes and place them 2 inches apart on the prepared baking sheets (we used a canapé cutter to cut

a small star in the middle of each large one). If you wish to hang the cookies, prick the top of each with the blunt end of a wooden skewer to create a hole. Gather up the dough scraps, form into a disk, and refrigerate again. Repeat to make more cookies.

3. Bake the cookies: Beat the remaining egg yolk and the cream in a small bowl. Brush the cookies very lightly with the egg wash. Bake, rotating the pans halfway through, until the cookies are golden brown—about 15 minutes. If you made holes, prick the cookies again when you rotate the pans to keep the holes open. Transfer the cookies to wire racks to cool completely. Store in an airtight container for up to 1 week.

125. SPITZBUEBE

These pretty cookies require a little work but they're worth it. The star cutout in the center of the top layer shows off the jam filling.

Makes 4 dozen cookies

2 cups unsalted butter
(4 sticks), softened

4 cups confectioners' sugar

4 large egg yolks

$4\frac{2}{3}$ cups all-purpose flour

1 cup seedless jam, warmed until syrupy

Confectioners' sugar for dusting

1. Make the dough: Beat the butter in a large bowl using an electric mixer set on medium speed until creamy. Gradually add the 4 cups confectioners' sugar and continue to beat until light and fluffy—5 to 8 minutes. Beat in the egg yolks, one at a time; then stir in the flour. Shape the dough into four $\frac{1}{2}$-inch-thick squares and wrap each in plastic wrap. Refrigerate for at least 45 minutes.

2. Bake the cookies: Preheat the oven to 350°F. Line 2 baking sheets with parchment paper. Set aside. Roll out one square of the dough on a lightly floured surface to $\frac{1}{4}$-inch thickness. Using 2-inch cutters, cut out an equal number of smooth and scalloped rounds. Then use a star cutter to punch out the centers on the scalloped rounds. Place the rounds on the prepared baking sheets. Reduce the oven temperature to 325°F and bake until golden—about 15 minutes. Repeat with the remaining dough and dough scraps. Transfer the cookies to wire racks to cool. Spoon $\frac{1}{4}$ teaspoon jam on each of the solid cookies. Dust the star-cut-out cookies with the remaining confectioners' sugar. Place the star-cut-out cookies on top of the jam-topped cookies. Store, layered between sheets of wax paper, in an airtight container for up to 1 week.

Photography credits

Numbers below indicate the page on which a photo appears.

Jim Bastardo: 77
John Bessler: 99
John Blais: 84
Kindra Clineff: 4 (bottom center), 25, 30 (right), 32, 33 (bottom), 35 (top, bottom left),
    39, 41 (bottom right), 45, 46, 47, 49, 51, 52, 69 (left)
Grey Crawford: 10, 38 (right), 44
Courtesy of Country Living: 85
Susie Cushner: 76
Christopher Drake: 65, 80
Christophe Dugied: 68 (right)
Charles Gold: 4 (bottom right), 106
Catherine Gratwicke: 81
John Gruen: 64 (left), 69 (right)
Philippe Kress: 89 (bottom)
Michael Luppino: 1, 12 (right), 83
Charles Maraia: 73 (left)
Andrew McCaul: 105
Susan Gentry McWhinney: 4 (bottom left), 12 (left), 22, 66, 72, 78
Maura McEvoy: 71 (left)
David Montgomery: 17
Keith Scott Morton: 2, 14, 15 (left), 18, 19, 20, 23 (left), 27, 41 (bottom left), 53, 54, 64
    (right), 82, 86, 87, 92, 103
Toshi Otsuki: 4 (top), 21, 42 (right), 43, 96, 104
Luciana Pampalone: 58
Christian Petersen: 68 (left)
David Prince: 13, 37, 61 (right), 71 (right), 73 (right)
Steven Randazzo: 3, 28, 29, 30 (left), 33 (top), 34, 36, 38 (left), 40, 48, 56, 59, 61 (left), 62,
    63, 70, 74, 89 (top), 91, 94, 95
Charles Schiller: 23 (right), 50
William P. Steele: 42 (left), 55, 88
Brooke Slezak: 31, 60, 114, 122
Ann Stratton: 67, 100, 108, 111, 112, 116, 117, 119, 120
Kristen Strecker, 15 (right)
Robin Stubbert: 8, 11, 16, 24, 26, 35 (bottom right), 41 (top), 97
James Worrell: 102

Index

HEARST BOOKS
New York

An Imprint of Sterling Publishing
387 Park Avenue South
New York, NY 10016

Copyright © 2011 by Hearst Communications, Inc.

This book was previously published as a hardcover under the title
Merry & Bright, 978-1-58816-636-4.

Book design: Jon Chaiet

Photography editor: Alexandra Brodsky

Library of Congress Cataloging-in-Publication Data
Country living : merry & bright : 125 festive ideas for celebrating Christmas / from the editors of Country Living.
     p. cm.
 Includes index.
 ISBN 978-1-58816-907-5
 1. Christmas decorations. 2. Handicraft. 3. Christmas cooking. I. Country living (New York, N.Y.) II. Title: Merry & bright. III. Title: Festive ideas for celebrating Christmas.
 TT900.C4C683 2011
 745.594'12--dc22

                    2011004518

10 9 8 7 6 5 4 3 2 1

www.countryliving.com

For information about custom editions, special sales, premium and corporate purchases, please contact Sterling Special Sales Department at 800-805-5489 or specialsales@ sterlingpublishing.com.

Distributed in Canada by Sterling Publishing
^c/o Canadian Manda Group, 165 Dufferin Street
Toronto, Ontario, Canada M6K 3H6

Distributed in Australia by Capricorn Link (Australia) Pty. Ltd.
P.O. Box 704, Windsor, NSW 2756 Australia

Manufactured in China

ISBN 978-1-58816-907-5

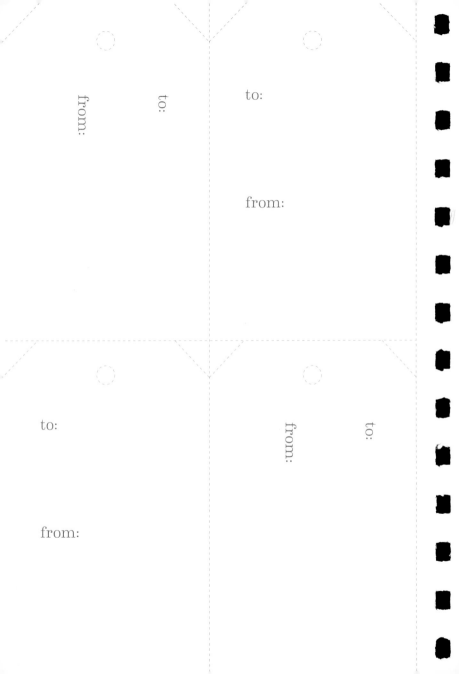

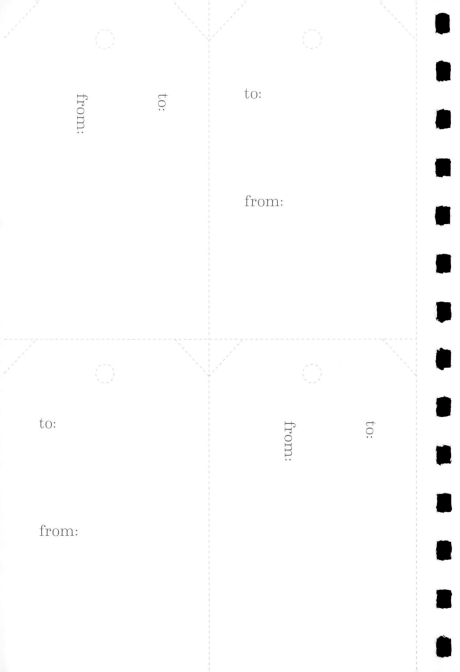

to:

from:

to:

from:

to:

from:

to:

from:

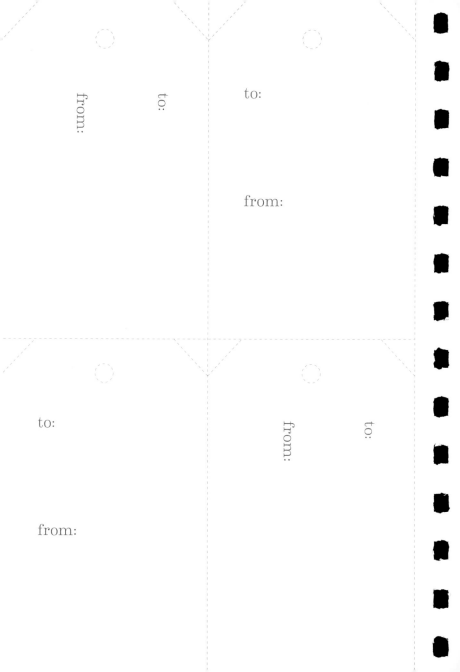

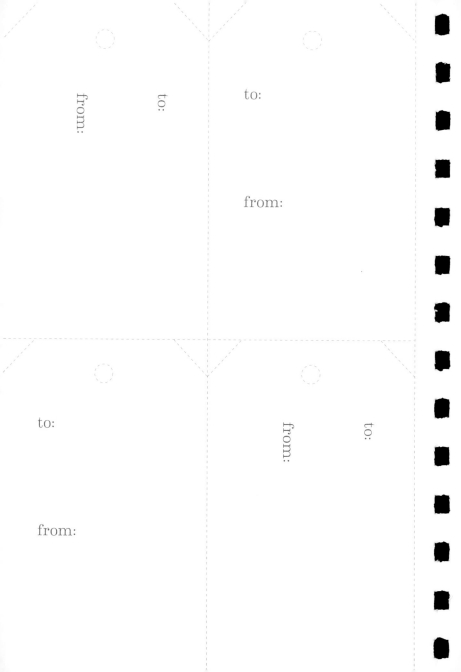

to:

from:

from:

to:

to:

from:

to:

from:

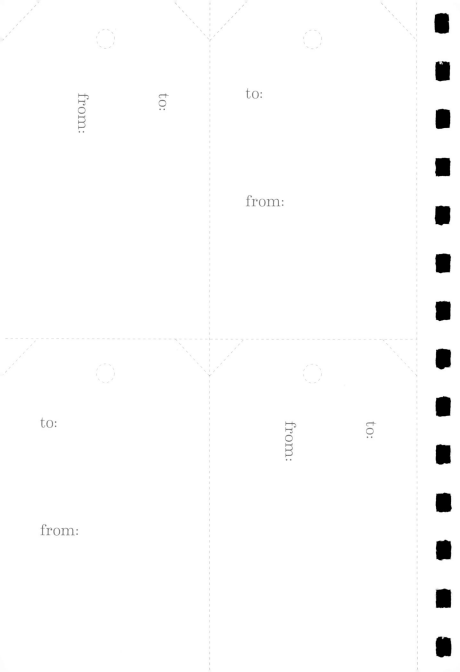

to:

from:

to:

from:

from:

to:

from:

to:

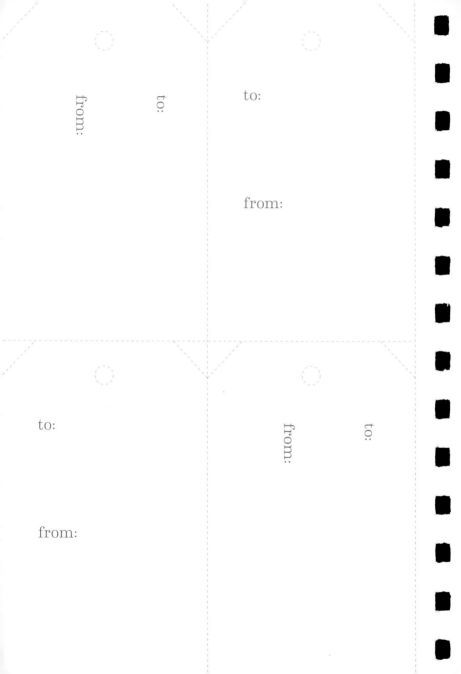

to:

from:

to:

from:

to:

from:

to:

from:

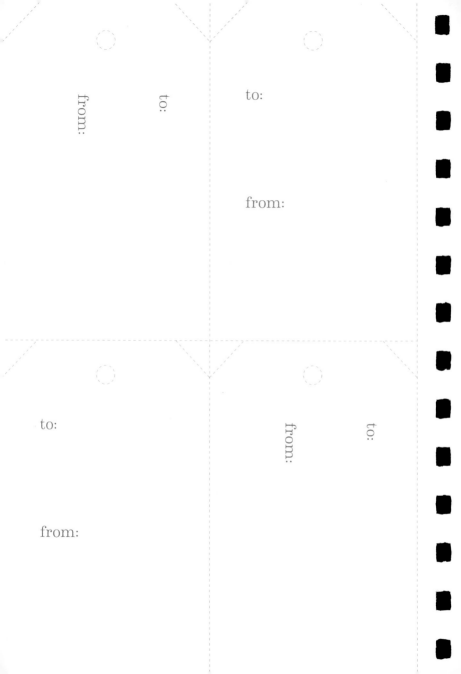

to:

from:

to:

from:

to:

from:

to:

from:

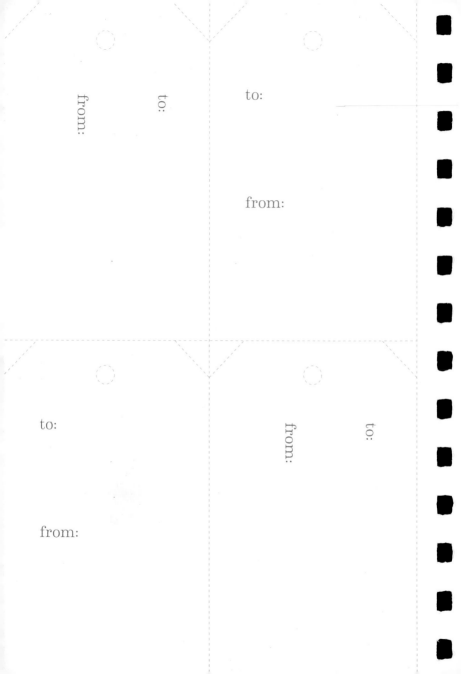

to:

from:

to:

from:

to:

from:

to:

from: